Profiles, Portfolios and How to Build Them

Jane McGrother RGN RNT MEd
Leader of Vocational Studies
Manchester College of Midwifery and Nursing

Illustrations by
Phil Mone

Scutari Press ● London

A division of RCN Publishing Company Ltd.

First published 1995

British Library Cataloguing in Publication Data

McGrother, Jane
    Profiles, Portfolios and How to Build Them
    I. Title
    650.14

ISBN 1 873853 38 6

Typeset by Scutari Press
Printed and bound in Great Britain

Library

Stepping Hill Hospital
Poplar Grove
Stockport SK2 7JF

Profiles, Portfolios and How to Build Them

Contents

Introduction: PREP requirements

Introduction

This booklet is about developing a professional profile or portfolio. It is aimed particularly at nurses; but for anyone thinking of building a portfolio of achievement the principles are the same. There are 650 000 nurses registered with the UKCC. In order to renew their registration these nurses must **now** fulfil the requirements outlined in the final PREP report (UKCC 1994). The purpose of Post Registration Education and Practice (PREP) is **'to improve standards of patient and client care...'** (UKCC 1995). It is your responsibility as a registered nurse to ensure that this happens and to document your professional development.

By now you will probably have received your copy of *Standards for Education Following Practice* (UKCC 1995). This is a pack of factsheets which provide definitive advice from the UKCC on what you should do and how to collect your profile. **Factsheet 1** in the pack describes **four** elements to maintaining your registration:

> • You will be required to 'complete a Notification of Practice form every three years' to confirm that you are **a practising nurse.**
>
> • You must 'undertake a minimum of five days' **study** or equivalent every three years.'
>
> • You must 'maintain a **Personal Professional Profile** with details of your professional development.'
>
> • If you have been **out of practice** for five years or more, you must 'undertake a Return to Practice programme.'

This process commenced on **1 April 1995** with all practitioners in the new system by 31 March 2001 after which the UKCC will initiate an auditing system to monitor PREP policies.

Many practitioners are expressing anxiety over what a profile looks like. *What should be put in as evidence? What do I do with it? Who will look at it? How can I use it? Is it all a waste of time, just a gimmick?* This booklet aims to answer these questions and to suggest that far from being a waste of time, a portfolio can help you **plan** your career, **identify gaps** in your experience and education, **prepare** for an interview and provide a satisfying and rewarding **record** of your professional achievements.

If you are at the beginning of your career, start collecting **today;** if you are half-way through, don't throw anything away; if you are nearly at the end celebrate your achievements and put together a record you can be proud of.

The booklet begins with some definitions for clarification, suggests some exercises to help you along and provides examples of real life professionals who have been through the process of collecting their portfolios. All names have been changed to protect confidentiality. Finally, you may wish to use the content of your portfolio to seek academic credit or exemption from an academic course. Guidelines are provided to optimise your chances of having your claim recognised. Here again, real life examples have been provided.

2 Profile or portfolio?

Normally we talk about our profile as being the side view of our face; or we may think of those interviews with famous people in newspapers and magazines 'Profile of Mick Jagger' or 'Profile of Nelson Mandela'. *Chambers 20th Century Dictionary* (1983) defines 'profile' as 'a head or portrait in a side view' or, more significantly in the context of a professional profile: '... a short biographical sketch; ... an outline ... to the extent to which it reveals one's activities, feelings, intentions and involvement ...' The same dictionary defines portfolio as 'a case or pair of boards for loose papers, etc'. For convenience and to save papers falling all over the place a ringbinder is a cheap alternative.

The UKCC has chosen to use the term 'profile' in referring to its requirements. The intention with a professional profile is that you draw a **biographical sketch** of yourself as a developing professional individual. During the process you should record what path your professional development has taken, what led you to the choices you made, how you prepared yourself for your different roles within your profession and what you have learned about your job, your skills and needs and about yourself. More than anything, it should demonstrate how your professional updating has **improved the care of your client group.**

The UKCC will *not* be calling in your profile for examination as this would be too costly. The intention is to undertake 'a series of pilot studies' (UKCC 1995, *Factsheet 5*) after which a final formal system will be installed.

There are many commercial portfolios on the market with smart printed pages and ideas for what to put into them. Most of them are A4 size while some have been designed like personal organisers. Many have sections on life experiences as well as professional experiences but this is **not** essential for UKCC purposes. However, you can build your own with a plain ringbinder and plastic pockets available cheaply from any highstreet stationer. Plastic pockets will make your portfolio bulky as it grows, but they are useful for certificates which you do not want to damage by punching holes in them. Store the originals safely in a separate binder.

If you have access to a word processor and the skills to go with it then you can present your portfolio very smartly and individually. But remember, it is the evidence that is important not merely the presentation.

So how do I begin?

It may be useful to imagine that a stranger is looking at your profile and knows nothing about you. By the time they have finished reading it, they should be much better informed about your professional life, your successes and **what you have achieved** in your career.

First of all you need to say who you are, your address, telephone number, current workplace and PIN. If you are not using a commercial portfolio, make this a bold first page.

Professional Portfolio

Name: **PIN:**

Work Address:

Home Address:

Tel: Home: **Work:**

Your next page could identify your **qualifications** both academic and professional.

Academic Qualifications
e.g. 'O' & 'A' levels, GCSE, BTEC, City & Guilds, etc.

Qualification	Subject	Grade	Date obtained

Professional Qualifications
e.g. RGN, RMN, RNMH, RSCN, RM

Qualification	Date	Where obtained

Collect all your **certificates** together. These may include your school exam certificates if you wish or you could start with your professional qualifications if you prefer. You should include **certificates of attendance** on study days and the programmes if you still have them.

Now lay them out in **chronological** order. Think about yourself as you remember the times when you achieved them. How did they help you professionally? How did they help you to improve your practice? Write down how you are different now. Were there any particular experiences which changed your life or your perspective on your chosen career? Think of the good times as well as the more difficult moments. You may like to lay your pages out as below. Ask yourself the following questions.

Post-Registration Education
e.g. ENB courses, study days, conferences, distance learning pack, night school (if relevant to your work, e.g. counselling)

Subject of course/study day

Validating body

Date attended

What I learned

How I have used the learning in my work?

How do I develop my portfolio further?

Be positive while you undertake this exercise. Enjoy the good memories and reflect on how you have coped with the difficult ones. Altogether, have you been successful in your terms?

This may not mean being the boss or earning lots of money. It may be that you have coped bravely with adversity or that you have learned something about yourself; that you have brought up a family or you are comfortable with yourself.

3 How do I develop my portfolio further?

Part of your portfolio should contain evidence of a factual nature which the UKCC will require (UKCC 1995, *Factsheet 4*). You need to keep a record of your **working hours** over the three year period between registrations. This could be incorporated into a section which looks at your **employment record and the development of your knowledge and skills.** This exercise will help you focus on your career and the posts you have held. Make a list of all the **posts,** the **grades** and the **responsibilities** you have held since you qualified. Note whether they were full-time or part-time.

Take a few minutes to think about your work and how it has changed over that time. Write down some of the **changes** you have observed.

The health service has experienced many changes in recent years both in delivering care and in the structure of the organisations such as the NHS and Social Services. Many of these changes have come about as a result of government White Papers such as *Working for Patients* (DoH 1989).

How have **you** adapted to the changes? How do you feel about them? Perhaps you have moved out of the NHS. Write down a few sentences to describe how you feel. Has the organisation you work for been affected in any way by all these changes? How have you kept up to date while these changes have been taking place? What do you read to help you keep up to date? Do you read a quality newspaper?

Make a list of the **professional journals** you are familiar with. Can you name the last article you were particularly interested in? What

Professional Experience to Date

Post held

Dates

Grade

Hours

Employer

Key responsibilities

What I learned

Any changes to practice I have introduced

was the significance to you and your work? Do you belong to an interest group or a working party etc? Write down all the **committees** and **groups** you have participated in. Do you have copies of the **minutes?** Put them in your portfolio.

EXAMPLE

Gillian took part in a working party which was looking at a standard for the administration of oxygen in her hospital. The group was multi-disciplinary and Gillian both contributed to the discussion and learned from the other group members. The minutes of those meetings and the work Gillian undertook as her share went into her portfolio.

---

4 Strengths and weaknesses

In these turbulent times it is useful to take stock of where we are in our lives. An exercise which you may be familiar with is the **SWOT** exercise. Make four lists under the headings **strengths, weaknesses, opportunities and threats.**

Strengths	Weaknesses
1. I have the relevant ENB awards	1. I am reluctant to address difficult situations
2. I have five years' experience in this specialty	2. I have difficulty in saying no
Opportunities	**Threats**
1. A re-organisation means an opportunity to apply for promotion	1. The reorganisation may result in a skillmix review and possible redundancy
2. The skillmix review will lead to training opportunities	2. New responsibilities could lead to stress, fatigue and neglecting my daughter

What are your strengths? What are you good at? What aspects of your character do you like best? How do these contribute to you being a good nurse and member of a team? Write down at least five things you are pleased about in yourself.

What are your weaknesses? What annoys you about yourself? What blocks to being a good team player do you experience? Write down five things about yourself you would like to change.

What are the **threats** to your wellbeing and professional role which disturb you most? Do they come from outside yourself? Do you see them as part of the turmoil in the health service and beyond your control? Is it something you do or not do which is part of the threat? Write down three things which you consider to be a threat to your job or happiness.

What are the **opportunities** in your life? Can you develop your existing skills and become an expert in your field? Is there a job you have yearned for but have not had the nerve to apply for? Can a threat be turned into an opportunity? For example: reorganisation of your workplace can be both a threat to your wellbeing and an opportunity to develop a new role. Can you take control? Write down three things you could do to improve your performance or your chances in the future jobmarket.

Having undertaken this exercise, now is the time to set some goals for yourself. Draw three columns on a sheet of paper. Head the columns: **goal, target date, date achieved.**

Begin by setting yourself **three goals.** Keep these simple to begin with so that you gain the satisfaction of achievement. For instance, try to finish each job before starting a new one; spend an hour reading to the children; spend one hour per week looking after yourself; speak to Mrs Smith's relatives whom you have been avoiding; be pleasantly assertive with that senior colleague; spend one hour in the library seeking some literature on a topic of your interest. Your goals should arise out of your self-appraisal just as if you were assessing a patient or client.

Now give yourself a **target date** by which to achieve your goal. When you have achieved it fill in the third column and reward yourself. This could be with a gold star although it is more likely to be with a feeling of satisfaction.

Goal	Target Date	Date Achieved
1. Spend one hour a night reading to the children	1. Two weeks	
2. Speak to S/N Smith about her behaviour towards junior staff	2. The next time we work together	
3. Go swimming once a week	3. For three weeks	

Now move on to **professional and/or career targets.** Is there a change to practice you would like to implement in your work area? Have you spoken to your manager? Have you looked into the need or justification for the change? What did you read to support your contention that change is needed? Have you produced a report/plan to support your case? All these questions could be answered by setting goals and targets for yourself. If you have written reports for your manager, put them in your portfolio.

On a grander scale; where would you like to be in two–five years' time? Have you seen a niche in the employment market?

Have you investigated the direction in which your area of expertise is moving? Are there **further qualifications** you need? Do you need to be working towards a diploma/degree? Could you manage a modular course which would fit in with your working and home life?

These are major goals which involve **long-term planning and foresight.** Your manager should be willing to discuss your future with you and what plans there are to develop the service you offer. Your target dates will be well ahead and you will need to talk to a College to discuss pathways to achieve them. One possibility is the ENB Framework and Higher Award leading to BSc(Hons) in Nursing. Think of the satisfaction as you tick off each stage in your plan.

EXAMPLE

Richard, an RSCN, became aware that a government directive required that there must be an RSCN in all Accident and Emergency departments. Richard set himself the goal of gaining a place on an ENB 199 course in Accident and Emergency Nursing. He asked for an informal interview with the College running the course, discussed his educational and professional plans and made out his case for attending the course even though he did not currently work in the A&E department. He was offered a place.

---

5 Five days' study every three years

Many nurses undertake far more than the required five days already and any formal course such as an ENB course or Diploma and Degree courses will qualify, providing they are **related to your professional development.** *It is up to you to justify that relationship.* The UKCC has not 'approved' any particular courses or study days although there will be many such opportunities offered to you by colleges. You may be able to use **night classes** as examples of professional updating if you have had a professional reason for embarking upon them.

EXAMPLE

One Community nurse began working in an area of her city with a high proportion of Asian families. In order to communicate effectively with her client group and provide sound nutritional advice for the parents of children, she attended night classes in Asian cookery. Her argument was that she needed to know what different Asian families eat before she could talk to them in a way they could appreciate.

Another nurse learned Urdu for similar reasons; yet another used her hobby of flower-arranging in her care of the elderly day centre to stimulate conversation and interest in her confused client group. Perhaps you have introduced your amateur dramatics, choir singing, musical evenings and/or juggling into your workplace. As long as you can claim **benefits for your client group** this may count as professional development. *It is up to you to make the claim.* One page of explanation in your portfolio would make out your case (UKCC 1995, *Factsheet 4*).

As you can see, professional development need not cost a great deal. A visit to another clinical area to look at how they deliver care would qualify. You would need to record the time spent, your objectives for the visit, your findings and reflections and whether you would recommend any action back in your own workplace. This could all be described in a brief report for your manager who may have supported your visit in the first place. Then the report goes in your portfolio.

EXAMPLE

Mary felt she needed to spend a day in the library looking up references to a new procedure which was to be introduced by the medical staff. She felt that a small learning package was needed by the staff and she was willing to produce it. Mary recorded the details of her time spent in the library, she kept a record of the references she found and put details of the teaching package in her portfolio. Her manager confirmed in writing that she had undertaken the project and that testimonial also went into her portfolio.

Time spent reading a professional journal could be recorded in your portfolio as personal development. You should make a record of the time spent and a brief résumé of any articles which were of particular relevance or interest to you. It is useful to develop the habit of recording the details of such articles, e.g. the author, title of article, journal name and date of publication; you may wish to refer to it again and if you are studying or intend to take up formal studies in the future, these records will save you enormous amounts of searching time.

6 Reflective practice

One of the aims of professional portfolios is to encourage you to become a reflective practitioner. You will see that all the previous pages have emphasised the importance of thinking about yourself and your work. Many nurses will argue that they already are reflective practitioners, however, our everyday experience tells us that there are others who do not stop to consider what they do and the effect their actions have on those with whom they work.

The literature on Reflective Practice is growing steadily. Atkins (1993) offers a useful review of some of this literature helping the reader cut through what she describes as 'complex and abstract' material. She looks at the definitions and processes of reflection, drawing on various models to illustrate ways in which the individual can practice reflection.

Patricia Benner, an American nurse who encouraged nurses to examine how they moved *From Novice to Expert* (1984), collected many examples of nurses' experiences and descriptions of how they had progressed during their careers. She was concerned to demonstrate that nursing is a high level skill which should be recognised as such but that in order to achieve that recognition, nurses must begin to analyse and record their development.

Schön (1987) expresses the view that professionals will be subjected to external criticism and disapproval if we 'fail to respond to value conflicts' or 'violate our own ethical standards' (p. 7). As nurses we should be regularly reviewing what we do and why we do it.

THE REFLECTIVE PRACTITIONER

How do I nurse?
How well do I do it?
Where is the evidence?
What can I change?
How do I change?
What do I need to know?

Performance review
Critical thinking
Discussion
Reflection
Research
Reading

Professionals have a body of knowledge based on scientific, research-based theories and concepts. What the nursing profession is building, however, on its own is not enough. There must be a relationship of understanding and trust between professionals and service users. In the field of health care this trust is the foundation of good practice.

Reflection in and on practice may enable us to enhance our relationships and the care we deliver. Greenwood (1993) warns against the risk of separating theory from practice and suggests that nurses are in danger of holding a theoretical opinion while practising something different. She uses the example of the theory that each client is an individual with their own special needs, but that in practice those needs are subordinated to the routine of the institution and the workload or attitudes of professionals. So, we say one thing and do another.

One approach to reflective practice is to consider an event which has occurred in your working life. Some writers call this a 'critical incident' while others prefer to use the term 'significant event' as this seems more positive.

Think of something which happened during the last three to four weeks and use a page of your profile to record events and your thoughts. You need only show it to those with whom you wish to share your thoughts.

You may find that as you think about what happens in your daily working life you come to recognise a shortcoming in your knowledge or skills. Congratulations! You are developing self-awareness. Now you need to do something about it.

Perhaps you need to do some reading, negotiate with your manager to enrol on one of the ENB courses or borrow a distance learning pack from the College library. You may find that some of your colleagues would like to join you in a study group.

However, don't forget to record the good things that happen too.

REFLECTIVE PRACTICE

Description of the event and who took part.

How did you feel about the part you played?

What would you do differently if something similar happened again?

What learning need have you identified for yourself?

7 Further questions to ask yourself

What were the circumstances which led up to the event? What happened? What was the outcome? Was the outcome beneficial to all concerned? What was my part in the outcome? Would I do anything differently if this event or something like it occurred again? Has this event highlighted a learning need in either myself or my colleagues? How can we satisfy that learning need?

These questions are **neutral** in the sense that they can be asked of both happy and unhappy events. They are intended to provide a framework for reflection, they are not intended to be a third degree grilling for yourself or your colleagues. You may then wish to discuss the issue with the colleagues involved. Try to look at the event as an idea sitting in the middle of a circle belonging to no-one in particular. It can then be reviewed by all concerned. Praise given liberally will raise self-esteem, motivate and empower. Supportive, constructive criticism can lead to enhanced responsibility and accountability.

EXAMPLE

Christine had a disagreement with a colleague. Normally, Christine would have stormed off in a huff. This time she paused and went away wondering if there was a better way to deal with this situation. She decided to write down what had occurred. This gave her time to reflect and the next day she approached her colleague and asked to talk the problem through. The issue was resolved and both of them felt better about the event.

---

8 Using your portfolio to prepare for an interview

> **EXAMPLE**
>
> David applied for a new post as an F grade staff nurse on a paediatric ward with a mixture of surgical disciplines. The ward has student nurses from Project 2000. He studied the advertisement carefully to help him identify the skills and knowledge he would need to demonstrate at the interview. David had been keeping a portfolio for two years. Two days before the interview he decided to go through his portfolio to look back on his role and achievements. He had the appropriate qualifications RSCN and ENB 998.
>
> ● David found the induction programme he had devised in his previous post to help all newcomers to the ward including a special section for students. He also had a teaching package for students on perioperative care.
>
> ● He had taken part in a standard setting group and had the minutes of the meetings and the final standard in his portfolio.
>
> ● As a personal exercise, David had conducted a literature search on the management of pain in children during a period when he felt it was not being managed well. He had written a brief résumé of his findings which he had presented to the ward team.
>
> ● Finally, in his portfolio, David found some reflections he had recorded of three satisfying periods during the past two years and two reflections on events which had caused him some heartache at the time.

At the interview, David was asked:

1. *Can you tell us about how you see your role as facilitator to new students coming onto the ward?*

David was able to talk about his induction programme and how useful it was in settling students and new staff into the ward.

2. *What is the role of F grades in maintaining the quality of care?*

To display his understanding of the importance of standards, David could recount his involvement in the setting of standards in his previous role and give examples of the standards which he and his colleagues found useful.

3. *What special expertise will you bring to the role of paediatric nurse?*

David has developed a special interest in the management of pain in children and babies. During his study of the subject he has found that this is a neglected area in the care of children. During the interview he will describe how his findings led to discussions with the medical staff and the improvement in the management of pain on his ward.

4. *Can you tell us about an event you were involved in which went well and another which went badly? What was the part you played in these events and what lessons did you learn?*

David was able to talk fluently about his experiences and achievements because they were fresh in his mind.

David is an imaginary character, but all these questions are the sort that you might be asked at interview and most good interviewers are looking for initiative, fluency and a sign of professional enthusiasm for the job. There may not be a 'right' answer to the question, this is your opportunity to sell yourself.

All of this section has been about providing evidence to satisfy the PREP requirements for you to be a thoughtful, developing, up-to-date practitioner. The next section shows you how you can use your portfolio to gain academic credit.

APL/APEL

Most of us realise that we learn a great deal outside the formal classroom environment. One only has to look at a fit and healthy one year old contemplating a staircase to recognise that the joy of learning begins at a very early age. Indeed, you may feel that you really began to learn about nursing after you were qualified and working in the real world.

Accreditation of Prior Learning (APL) is a way of recognising and giving credit for learning which may be otherwise **uncertificated**. This could include courses you have been on in the past. Experiential learning is what you learn through experience and is usually **unrecorded**. A system which includes **Accreditation of Prior Experiential Learning (APEL)** may enable you to gain credit for this previously unrecorded learning. If your claim is successful you will be awarded a certain number of **credit points** at a given level.

The great advantage of APL is that it saves you duplicating learning which you have already achieved. It can also recognise achievement and developments in the workplace and Simosko (1991) believes it encourages workers to maintain lifelong learning.

The disadvantages are that some people believe that only formal teaching can maintain standards and educational institutions will not always recognise credit points awarded by another college. You probably need to find college with an APL system and continue your studies with them. Also, **APL is not an easy option,** it can be time consuming and you need to be an **independent learner.**

The following pages describe the way in which you can make a claim and the criteria by which your portfolio will be assessed.

There are some principles to any APL system which are important to grasp:

- You must contact a college and ask about making a claim for credit.

- There is no formal teaching but you should receive tutorials to help you produce suitable evidence.

- You cannot just say you have had 10 years' experience; you must demonstrate learning has taken place.

- You must present a portfolio of evidence.

- Your portfolio must be assessed against a set of criteria.

- Your evidence must be professionally relevant.

- Your evidence must be of the appropriate academic level and this must be sufficient to justify the credit points you wish to claim.

Pathway to Accreditation of Prior Learning

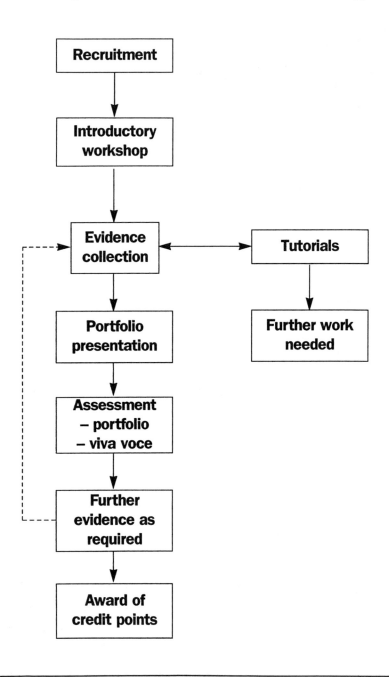

10 Claim examples

There are many activities which you may have been involved in for which you could claim credit if you present your evidence in a manner which satisfies the academic criteria.

Standard setting

Has your ward team devised and introduced a standard into your working area? Did everything go smoothly? How did you find time to discuss the standard setting? What literature did your group use to support the standard being set? What model did you use? Have you kept minutes of the meetings? How do you make sure everyone knows the standard and adheres to it? How is it measured? and so on.

Introducing a new piece of equipment to your working area

Has your workplace acquired a new piece of equipment recently? How was the decision taken to buy it? Who decided it was needed? What evidence was used to decide it was needed? How were you and your colleagues prepared for its use? Has it been beneficial to patient/client care? How do you know?

Introducing a change in practice to your workplace

Have you been on a study day or course where you learned something new which you wanted to implement in your own workplace? How did you set about introducing it to your colleagues and persuade them that this was the 'best idea since sliced bread'? Did you have any resistance? What evidence did you use to support your convictions? How did things go? Have you been successful?

A teaching package for your workplace

Have you produced a learning/teaching pack for your workplace? Why did you choose that particular subject? How did you go about designing and preparing it? What literature did you use to support the information in the pack? Where is it kept? Who uses it?

For some of these examples you may already have a large amount of evidence tidied away in files and cupboards. You will need to sort it out and organise it into a logical and presentable format.

You will almost certainly need to write an account of the evidence, explaining what it is all about, the problems you encountered and how you overcame them, if you did.

It is not essential for an attempt at change to be successful for you to have learned from the experience. If it was not successful you need to analyse why and say what you would do differently the next time. It is essential that you read around the subject and use the literature in your account.

11 Tutorials

You should be offered **tutorials** to assist you in preparing your evidence to the level required. The purpose of the tutorial is for you to receive advice about the **presentation** of your evidence. *It is not a teaching session,* nor is the teacher obliged to provide you with written materials such as articles or books, although the teacher may suggest some reading to help you. The better prepared you are when you arrive for your tutorial, the more benefit you will gain from the discussion.

12 Peer study groups

If you know others who are applying for APL why don't you consider starting a **support group?** Sharing ideas may lead you to include something in your portfolio which you previously considered insignificant.

Preparing for APL is not necessarily an easy option to formal study. It still requires commitment and organisation. However, the fact that it is based in your **clinical practice** means it is very relevant to you and your colleagues. You could all benefit from working together.

13 Assessment of the portfolios

When you and your teacher have decided that your portfolio is ready for submission, you will hand it in for marking.

A number of people will look at it in order to judge the level and number of **credit points** it can be awarded. Hopefully they will agree with your claim. If it is felt that you have not quite fulfilled the criteria, **recommendations** will be made about what you need to do further to satisfy the panel.

First level nurses are already awarded 60 level 1 credit points for their **registration qualification.** Many of you will find another 60 from study days and activities you have undertaken during your clinical career with help from your teacher/adviser. Most of you will be seeking to claim at level 2.

The final decision on your claim rests with the **examining body** of the educational institution through whom you are making your claim. Credit points are awarded for assessed work which is comparable to that undertaken during an undergraduate degree course. Thus:

    120 credit points at level 1 = Certificate   +
    120 credit points at level 2 = Diploma   +
    120 credit points at level 3 = Degree (Hons)

Credit points may be either **general** or **specific.** Specific credit points are awarded for exemption from particular (specific) courses. General credit points are given for achievements which may not be directly related to the course of study for which you are seeking credit but which may be seen as demonstrating ability. In practice it is wise to try to **match** your APL claim against an identified course or module. This makes it simpler for institutions to offer credit or exemption from parts of their programmes. Some of the examples in the next section may help to clarify this procedure.

14 Assessing the level of work in your portfolio

Candidates applying for APL will normally be encouraged to present the evidence of their learning in **creative and flexible** ways. However, in order to be awarded credit points for your learning, you must show that you have achieved at **a recognisable academic level.** Colleges have different ways of measuring the quality of the work which you submit but the following descriptions of achievement will provide you with a rough idea of what educational institutions will be looking for.

At **Level 1** the evidence in your portfolio will demonstrate knowledge, understanding and application of your learning to your daily work. You should show that you have read widely and that you can integrate theory with practice.

At **Level 2** you must show that you are beginning to analyse what you are learning in its relationship to practice or your personal development. You should be able to challenge existing practice where appropriate and demonstrate problem solving skills while using the literature to analyse your learning critically.

Finally, at **Level 3** you need to show that you have used your learning creatively to implement a change in practice or in your own behaviour and be able to justify the change. You will be able to evaluate the impact of the (attempted) change on those concerned, including clients, colleagues, yourself and/or your organisation and evaluate research findings using them appropriately to enhance patient/client care (see the following examples).

EXAMPLE ONE

Susan is a Clinical Nurse Specialist working in Accident and Emergency. She has undertaken several post-registration courses during her career and now wishes to gain credit for her previous learning as part of the ENB Framework and Higher Award BSc(Hons) Professional Studies in Nursing. For this degree, Susan needs 120 credit points at levels 1, 2 and 3 each. She has 8 years' experience in A&E, four of those as a senior nurse.

Susan is an RGN, has completed ENB 199, Accident and Emergency Nursing, ENB 998, Teaching and Assessing in Clinical Practice and a BTEC Continuing Education Management course, none of which were credited at the time she completed them.

Susan submits a portfolio containing;

1. reports written for managers on issues related to the provision of A&E services namely;

- need for children's play area

- investigation of need to provide post-coital contraception at weekends

- various changes to clinical practices

2. assignments undertaken on the BTEC course

3. health promotional materials

4. teaching/learning packages

To lift the academic level of her work, Susan had to provide additional written material in the form of assignments/essays to support her claim for level 2 credit points. The additional work was all based on her **previous** achievements and consisted of evaluating changes made and analysing the effects of the changes on all concerned.

The portfolio satisfied the criteria and was assessed as being worthy of 120 credit points at level 1 and 90 credit points at level 2. This is matched against the 60 level 2 points which the new ENB 199 carries, 15 level 2 points for Susan's management role matched against the Management module and 15 against the ENB 998 Teaching and Assessing in Clinical Practice.

Susan lacks any evidence of achievement in research knowledge and skills and is advised to undertake the Research Methods module at level 2 to complete 240 credit points. She will then need to acquire 120 credit points at level 3 through the normal channels of taught modules/courses to complete her BSc(Hons) and Higher Award.

EXAMPLE TWO

David is a Charge Nurse on an Orthopaedic ward. He is an RGN and has completed a Diploma in Nursing Studies but he does not have the ENB 219 which he needs for the progress of his professional career. All his assignments on his Diploma course were related to his Orthopaedic workplace.

David submitted a portfolio which matched his previous academic studies and achievements to the learning outcomes of the ENB 219 Orthopaedic Nursing. (This must include evidence of achieving the practice outcomes).

The portfolio was assessed as meeting the outcomes of the ENB course and David was recommended for the award of the ENB 219.

EXAMPLE THREE

Janet is a Practice Nurse. She wishes to progress her studies toward achieving at least a Diploma in Professional Studies in Nursing. She may consider going on to work for a degree in a few years when her family life is more settled but in the meantime she recognises that Practice Nurses will soon be required to demonstrate the ability to perform (at minimum) at Diploma level.

Janet attended the practice nurse course before it was credited and has developed protocols and auditing tools for screening clinics. In addition, she has undertaken an asthma course and a diabetes course for practice nurses. She had written essays for these courses but they did not demonstrate analysis nor had she used the literature in support of her arguments.

Janet was advised to read the current literature on auditing and to write an account of how these clinics were benefiting her local client population. The accounts need to show that she is able to propose a case supporting her arguments with the literature. She should show that she has taken into account the targets set by government documents and she should demonstrate some analysis of the socio-political issues involved. Janet conducted similar reviews of her other areas of practice.

Janet will need to enhance her written evidence to ensure that it reaches level 2 standard and can then claim credit points matched against the courses that the College runs.

In this case Janet was awarded 120 level 1 and 70 level 2 credit points. Janet worked in close collaboration with her College in order to be assured that the pathway she was undertaking would lead to her chosen goal. Unless this is done, you can accumulate much more than 120 credit points at the appropriate level, costing time and money.

National Vocational Qualifications (NVQs)

Many of you will be familiar with NVQs through working with candidates in your clinical practice. This is not the place to give detailed information about NVQ schemes and programmes, however, it is worth mentioning that portfolios are the method by which evidence is presented for the achievement of an NVQ. The performance criteria are very specific and designed to demonstrate competence, not necessarily academic credit, but it is possible that the evidence in your portfolio/profile for PREP purposes can also be used as part of a claim towards an NVQ.

Keep all information tidily, logically and well identified. It will then become easier to cross reference it for specific purposes. Your portfolio is your evidence of being an up to date, developing practitioner with insight and a range of skills and knowledge. Enjoy collecting it.

References

Atkins S (1993) Reflection: A review of the literature. *Journal of Advanced Nursing* 18: 118–1192

Benner P (1984) *From Novice to Expert: Excellence and Power in Clinical Nursing Practice.* California: Addison Wesley

Boud D, Keogh R and Walker R (eds) (1985) *Reflection: Turning Experience into Learning.* London: Kogan Page

Greenwood J (1993) Reflective practice: A critique of the work of Argyris and Schön. *Journal of Advanced Nursing* 18: 1183–1187

Schön D (1987) *Educating the Reflective Practitioner.* San Francisco: Jossey-Bass

Simosko S (1991) *APL: Accreditation of Prior Learning: A Practical Guide for Professionals.* London: Kogan-Page

UKCC (1994) *Post-Registration and Practice.* London: UKCC

UKCC (1995) *PREP and You.* PREP Factsheets. London: UKCC

Further reading

Brown RA (1992) *Portfolio Development and Profiling for Nurses.* Lancaster: Quay Publishing

Cameron BL and Mitchell AM (1993) Reflective peer journals: Developing authentic nurses. *Journal of Advanced Nursing* 18(2): 290–297

McGrother J (1993) Working for credit. *Nursing Times* 89(25): 34–35

McGrother J (1993) Keeping a high profile. *Nursing Times* 89(30): 40–42

Index